Ohio

By Christine Taylor-Butler

Subject Consultant
Erin Bartlett
Community and Support Services Coordinator, Western Region
Ohio Historical Society Museums Division
Columbus, Ohio

Reading Consultant
Cecilia Minden-Cupp, PhD,
Former Director of the Language and Literacy Program,
Harvard Graduate School of Edcation,
Cambridge, Massachusetts

Children's Press®
A Division of Scholastic Inc.
New York   Toronto   London   Auckland   Sydney
Mexico City   New Delhi   Hong Kong
Danbury, Connecticut

Designer: Herman Adler
Photo Researcher: Caroline Anderson
The photo on the cover shows the Cincinnati skyline.

Library of Congress Cataloging-in-Publication Data

Taylor-Butler, Christine.
  Ohio / by Christine Taylor-Butler.
    p. cm. — (Rookie read-about geography)
  Includes index.
  ISBN-13: 978-0-531-12573-1 (lib. bdg.)   978-0-531-16816-5 (pbk.)
  ISBN-10: 0-531-12573-4 (lib. bdg.)   0-531-16816-6 (pbk.)
  1. Ohio—Juvenile literature. 2. Ohio—Geography—Juvenile literature.
  I. Title. II. Series.
  F491.3.T39 2007
  977.1—dc22   2006017609

A buckeye tree

Do you know why Ohio is called the Buckeye State?

The buckeye is Ohio's state tree. The nuts on this tree look like the eyes of a buck, or deer.

Can you find Ohio on this map?

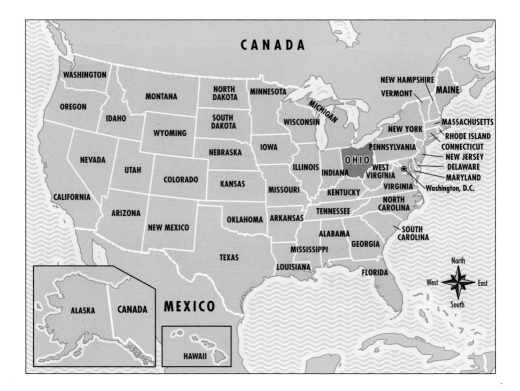

CANADA

WASHINGTON

OREGON

IDAHO

MONTANA

NORTH
DAKOTA

MINNESOTA

WYOMING

SOUTH
DAKOTA

WISCONSIN

MICHIGAN

NEVADA

UTAH

NEBRASKA

IOWA

COLORADO

KANSAS

CALIFORNIA

ARIZONA

NEW MEXICO

OKLAHOMA

ARKANSAS

TEXAS

MISSOURI

ILLINOIS

INDIANA

KENTUCKY

TENNESSEE

NEW HAMPSHIRE

VERMONT

MAINE

NEW YORK

MASSACHUSETTS

RHODE ISLAND

PENNSYLVANIA

CONNECTICUT

OHIO

NEW JERSEY

WEST
VIRGINIA

DELAWARE

MARYLAND

VIRGINIA

Washington, D.C.

NORTH
CAROLINA

SOUTH
CAROLINA

ALABAMA

GEORGIA

MISSISSIPPI

LOUISIANA

FLORIDA

ALASKA

CANADA

MEXICO

HAWAII

North

West   East

South

5

A cardinal

Ohio's state bird is
the cardinal.

The state flower is the
red carnation.

Long ago, large sheets of moving ice called glaciers covered Ohio. These glaciers flattened the land.

The Lake Plains Region in northern Ohio has the flattest land in the state.

A farm in Ohio's Lake Plains Region

Lake Erie

Lake Erie forms the northern border of Ohio. Bass, catfish, and yellow perch live in this freshwater lake.

Northeastern Ohio is filled with rolling hills and flat valleys. This area also has several small forests and lakes.

Corn growing on northeastern Ohio's rolling hills

A farmer works on a soybean farm in Ohio.

The Till Plains are located
in southwestern Ohio.
This area is excellent
for farming.

Many Ohio farmers grow
corn and soybeans.

A coal mine in southeastern Ohio

Southeastern Ohio has many steep hills and valleys. Miners often come here to dig up a mineral called coal.

Wayne National Forest is located in southeastern Ohio.

White-tailed deer, woodchucks, and turkeys live here.

A woodchuck

Native American mounds in Ohio

Thousands of years ago, ancient people built mounds in Ohio. Mounds are large piles of soil and stone.

Some of the mounds may have been used as graves. Many of the mounds are shaped like squares, circles, and even animals.

Columbus is Ohio's capital. It is also the largest city in the state.

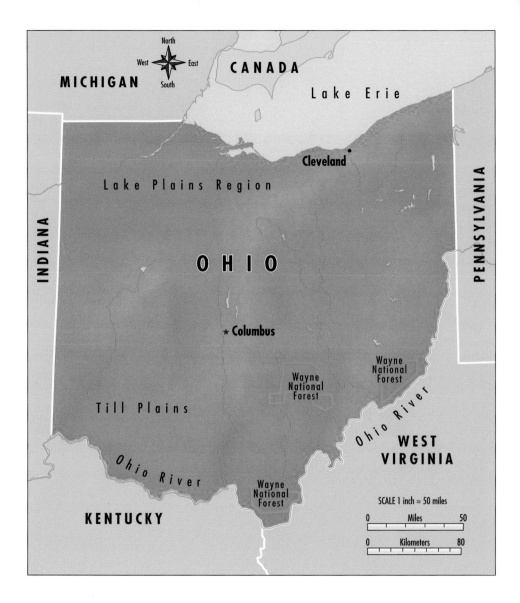

25

Cleveland's Rock and Roll Hall of Fame

Cleveland is another large city in Ohio.

The Rock and Roll Hall of Fame is located in Cleveland. This museum has exhibits on many famous musicians.

Maybe one day you will visit Ohio.

What will you do first when you get there?

Visitors to Ohio prepare for a sailboat ride.

Words You Know

buckeye

cardinal

Lake Erie

miners

mounds

Ohio River

soybeans

woodchuck

31

Index

About the Author

Christine Taylor-Butler is the author of twenty-eight books for children and is a native of Ohio. She is a graduate of the Massachusetts Institute of Technology and is also the author of five other books in the Rookie Reader Read-About® Geography series: *Hawaii, Kansas, Missouri, The Missouri River,* and *Vermont.*

Photo Credits

Photographs © 2007: Alamy Images/David R. Frazier Photolibrary, Inc.: 9, 14, 31 bottom left; AP/Wide World Photos/Scott Shaw/Plain Dealer: 18, 30 bottom right; Corbis Images/John Conrad: 21, 31 bottom right; Dembinsky Photo Assoc./Skip Moody: 6, 30 top right; Getty Images/Peter Pearson/Stone: cover; Ian Adams Photography: 10, 30 bottom left; Masterfile: 13 (Garry Black), 26 (Gail Mooney); Ohio Department of Natural Resources: 3, 29, 30 top left; Peter Arnold Inc./Matt Meadows: 22, 31 top left; Superstock, Inc.: 17, 31 top right.

Maps By Bob Italiano